ABCS OF CLOUD COMPUTING

A GUIDE TO ENTER THE WORLD OF CLOUD COMPUTING

DAVID LIVINGSTON J

Made with ♥ on the Notion Press Platform
www.notionpress.com

Contents

CHAPTER ONE

COMPUTING
PARADIGMS

The term **paradigm** refers to a set of practices to be followed to accomplish a task. In the domain of computing, **paradigm** refers to the standard practices to be followed for performing computing with the help of computing hardware and software. Along with all computing devices and the Internet, computing paradigms were also developed keeping pace with these advancements.

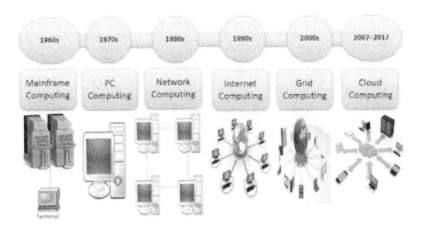

Fig. 1.1: Evolution of Computing Paradigms (1960 - 2017)

There are various **computing paradigms** available now-a-days that include the following:

1

1. High Performance Computing (HPC)
2. Network Computing
3. Cluster Computing
4. Grid Computing
5. Cloud Computing
6. Bio Computing
7. Mobile Computing
8. Quantum Computing
9. Optical Computing and
10. Nano Computing

High Performance Computing:

In High Performance Computing, systems are having a pool of processors (CPU) connected (networked) with other resources such as memory, storage, and input and output devices. The software deployed on a HPC system is normally enabled to run on the entire system of connected components. Examples of HPC include a small cluster of desktop computers or a super computer. They are generally used for solving scientific problems.

High Performance Computing makes use of any one of the following architectures for connecting devices in a network:

1. Server Architecture
2. Parallel Architecture
3. Distributed Architecture

While initially computing was perceived to be centralized, they were decentralized and distributed with the advent of Internet, client/server and parallel architecture. In **centralized computing paradigm**, all computer resources such as processors, memory, storage etc. are typically located in one physical system and controlled centrally.

In **server architecture**, computers are connected to a network that consists of one **server system** and multiple **client systems.** In this architecture, functionality of the system is split between two computers - a **server** and a **client**. The server satisfies the requests generated by client systems.

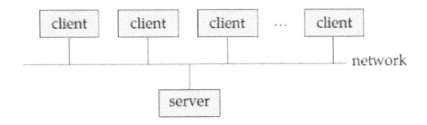

Fig. 1.2: Client/Server Architecture

Systems that deal with large number of users adopt a **three-tier architecture**, in which the front end is a **Web browser** which talks to an **application server** running remotely. The application server, in turn, talks to the **databaseserver** for storage and retrieval of data from a centralized database.Computing system that makes use of client/server or multi-tier architecture is also called as **Networked Computing**.

Parallel and Distributed Architecture

Parallel computing refers to the mechanism of a computer system, which makes it capable of running computations parallel or simultaneously by multiple CPUs. In **parallel architecture**, processing takes place in multiple CPU of the same computer, or in multiple processors of various computers that run simultaneously.

The processors (CPU) are mostly of homogeneous type in a parallel computer. All the processors running simultaneously share a central memory and communicate through a shared memory in a tightly coupled environment in a parallel computer. **Supercomputer** is an example of parallel computer, in which hundreds of thousands of processors are interconnected to solve a computational problem.

Parallel systems improve processing and I/O speed by using multiple CPUs and disks in parallel. In **parallelprocessing**, many operations are performed simultaneously as opposed to serial processing, in which the computational steps are performed sequentially. Given below are the major differences between a conventional computer (also called Serial computer) and a Parallel computer:

Characteristics of a Serial Computer:

1. Runs on a single Computer/processor machine having a single CPU
2. Given problem is broken down into a discrete set of instructions executed by a single CPU
3. Instructions are executed one after another

Characteristics of a Parallel Computer:

1. Runs multiple processors (CPU) simultaneously for executing a complex task
2. Given problem is broken down into discrete parts that can be processed concurrently by multiple CPUs
3. Each discrete part is further broken down into a set of instructions and are executed simultaneously on different CPUs, which are controlled by a special mechanism

There are two main measures of performance of a parallel computer that makes use of parallel processing: **through-put** and **response time**. **Through-put** refers to the number of tasks that can be completed in a given time interval and **response time** refers to the amount of time it takes to complete a single task from the time it is submitted.

Parallel Architecture:

There are several architecture models for parallel machines. The following are four architectures in which multiple processors are running parallel, and the resources such as memory, processor and databases are shared among them in four different ways:

1. **Shared Memory Architecture**: In this architecture, all the processors share a common memory.
2. **Shared Disk Architecture**: All the processors share a common set of disks and the shared-disks connected to this system are called **clusters**.
3. **Shared Nothing Architecture**: In this kind of architecture, the processors share neither a common memory nor common disk among themselves.

4. **Hierarchical Architecture**: In this model of parallel processing, a hybrid architecture that makes use of more than one of the above mentioned architecture is used.

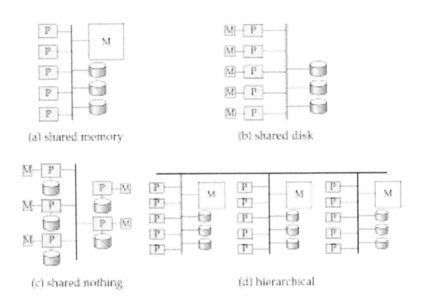

(a) shared memory   (b) shared disk

(c) shared nothing   (d) hierarchical

Fig. 1.3: Four Different Architectures of Parallel Computing

Cluster computing is a type of parallel computing, in which cluster of homogeneous computers are connected, which are cooperatively working together to accomplish a task that can't be easily solved by a serial computer.

Distributed Architecture:

Distributed computing paradigm consists of a collection of independent computers, each having its own memory and other capabilities, but cooperating with each other computers to solve a problem. The computers connected to the **distributed environment** communicate with one another through various communication media, such as high-speed networks or telephone lines.

The participating computers communicate with each other through message passing and the group appears to be a single coherent system to the users. The computers connected in a distributed system are referred to as **sites** or **nods**. Nodes do not share main memory or disks. They may also vary in size and function, ranging from workstations up to mainframe systems.

Distributed architecture looks similar to that of Shared Nothing Architecture in parallel systems. The main differences between distributed architecture and shared-nothing parallel architecture are the following:

1. Distributed systems are typically geographically separated
2. They are separately administered and
3. They may have a slower interconnection between the systems connected in the network

CHAPTER TWO

DISTRIBUTED & OTHER PARADIGMS

Distributed computing makes use of multiple computers or processor machines connected through a network, which can be homogeneous or heterogeneous, but run as a single system. The systems connected in a distributed computing environment may be located in the same building or in a place that is geographically dispersed.

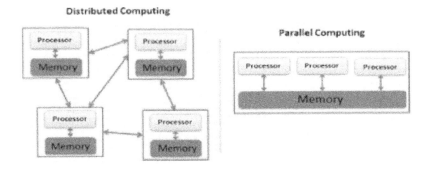

Fig. 2.1: Distributed Vs. Parallel Computing

The goal of distributed computing is to make computers of ranging from PC to workstations to minicomputers work together as a single system. The advantage of distributed computing over centralized systems are Scalability and Availability.

Cluster, Grid and Cloud Computing

Cluster Computing uses parallel architecture, especially **Shared Disk Architecture** for forming the Cluster that can be shared by multiple computers or processors (CPU) simultaneously. It makes use of a set of same or similar type of processor machines connected using a dedicated network infrastructure.

The individual Computer in a cluster can be referred to as **nodes**. Each and every node in a cluster shares a common storage and runs software such as **Message Passing Interface** (MPI) that allows programs to run across all nodes simultaneously.

All the nodes in a cluster work cooperatively using the software that implements MPI (Message Passing Interface) to solve the problem in hand. The advantage of using Cluster Computing is to allow each and every node to work together with other nodes to solve a complex problem that can't be easily solved by any PC with serial processing.

Grid Computing:

Grid computing uses Shared nothing Architecture of Parallel Computing for connecting multiple computers or processing machines that run parallelly. It is a kind of distributed computing in which underutilized computing resources of various organization can be made available to its users through some software that acts as the middleware between those resources available remotely.

The idea of grid computing is to make use of nonutilized computing power by the needy organization, and thereby Return on Investment (ROP) of those computing resources can be increased. The managing functions of resources available in a grid are known as grid services. Grid services provide following functionalities to grid users for effectively managing the resources available on the grid:

1. Access control
2. Security services
3. Data access which include accessing databases and digital libraries
4. Access to large-scale and long-term Storage facilities.

Grid computing is thus named because it looks similar to the electric Power Grid, in which the user doesn't need to know where the electricity comes from (source). There is a grid called **power grid** which acts as a mediator between the source of electricity and the end user. The power grid is made up of transmission stations, power stations, transformers, power lines etc.

Moreover, Power Grid allows its users to avail power (electricity) as a utility. We ask for electricity and we get it; we also pay for what we get and utilize. Similarly, in Grid Computing, Grid provides the Infrastructure and necessary mechanism for accessing computing resources which are available in the form of PC, workstation and servers along with storage elements. In grid computing, we ask for computing power or storage capacity and we get it.

Cloud Computing:

Cloud Computing is a internet-based paradigm, in which shared resources available to end-users on an on-demand basis. Cloud computing is a kind of Distributed Computing, in which computing power is made available to end users as a utility with a help of various concepts of distributed computing that include virtualization, utility computing, Service Oriented Architecture (SOA) etc.

The difference between grid Computing and cloud computing is that grid computing supports leveraging several computing and storage devices in parallel to solving a particular problem, while cloud computing supports leveraging multiple resources which are available in one or more data centres to deliver a unified service to the end user. The resources available in large data centres are provided in the form of services to either an individual or general public

Mobile & Other Computing Paradigms

In mobile computing handheld devices are used for processing and they communicate with each other through wireless medium. This includes smart phones, tablets, smart watches, and other portable devices that users interact with.

Mobile Ecosystem refers to the networking infrastructure, technologies and services that enable end users to make use of mobile computing and communication. The mobile ecosystem has become a fundamental part of modern life, impacting how we communicate, work, learn, and interact with the world around us. Some of the useful applications of mobile computing include:

1. Voice communication
2. Sending and receiving messages
3. Video call or conferencing
4. Sending and receiving money using applications online

The users of mobile computing environment will be able to access data and applications from any device and on any network while on the move. While on the move, the preferred device will be a mobile device, while back at home or in the office the device could be a desktop computer. To make the mobile computing environment ubiquitous (seeming to be everywhere or in several places at the same time), it is necessary that the communication bearer is spread over both wired and wireless media.

Bio Computing:

Examples include DNA computing, which utilises DNA's structure for data storage and manipulation, and cellular computing, in which programs make use of biological cells to perform computational tasks. Bio Computing refers to the user of biological systems like DNA or cells to perform computations. It's a field that seeks to harness the computational capabilities of biological molecules and systems, going beyond traditional silicon-based computers.

Bio Computing Systems make use of biologically derived or simulated molecules (or modules) that perform computational processes in order to solve a problem. The biologically derived models aid in structuring the computer program that becomes part of the application. Using the concepts and techniques defined in this computing, scientists can explore proteins and DNA, which are the basic building blocks of the nature.

Optical computing:

Optical computing, also known as **photonic computing**, is a revolutionary computing paradigm that utilises **light waves (photons)** instead of electrical signals (electrons) for data processing, storage, and communication. Photons can transmit data much faster than electrons, potentially leading to significantly increased computational speeds.

Optical computing system uses the photons in visible light or infrared beams, rather than electric current to perform computations. Instead of manipulating electron flow in silicon chips, optical computing manipulates the properties of light, such as intensity, phase, polarization, and wave length, to encode and process information.

Optical computing also takes advantage of visible and/or IR networks at the device and component level, which will result in a system that runs 10 times or more faster than a conventional electronic computer. Optical fibre is the medium of communication used for data transmission over long distances in optical computing.

Quantum Computing:

Quantum computing is an advanced form of computation that leverages the principles of **quantum mechanics** to solve complex problems that are intractable for even the most powerful classical computers. Quantum computing is built using quantum-based solutions that replaces Integrated Circuits (ICs) with quantum-based chips for increasing the speed of the processing, further.

Quantum computers can work much more faster than that of the super computers. At the most fundamental level itself, quantum computing works differently than that of the existing conventional (serial) and parallel systems. Although they are available in the form of prototype, they have not been proved to be an alternative for today's silicon based machines.

Qubits (Quantum Bits): This is a concept newly introduced in Quantum Computing for the storage and processing of data. Unlike classical bits which can only be either 0 or 1, qubits can exist in a **superposition** of both 0 and 1 simultaneously. This means a single qubit can hold more information than a classical bit.

Nano Computing:

Nano computing refers to computing system that are constructed using nano scale components. In this type of computing systems, computers are made up of transitions constructed using carbon nano tubes instead of silicon transistors which are generally used in the construction of traditional computers.

The successful realisation of nano computers totally depend on the nano scale and integration of nano tubes in forming the transistors. Nano computing face two major issues in bringing this computing paradigm into reality:

1. Issues of scale
2. Issues of integration

The issues of scale is related to the dimensions of the components; they are, at most, a few nano meters in at least two dimension. The issues of integration of the components are twofold:

1. The manufacture of complex arbitary patterns may be economically infeasible
2. Nano computers may include massive quantities of devices

CHAPTER THREE

INTRODUCTION TO CLOUD COMPUTING

Every aspect of the computer has gone through a sea of change during the past fww decades. However, with these changes came the problem of scalability. As we grow or increase in one area, the other related areas must also be able to grow accordingly to accommodate the changes.

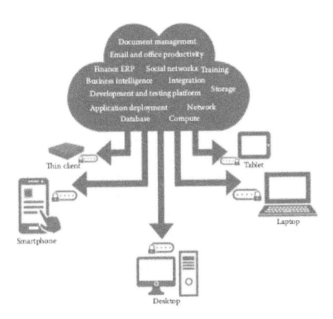

Fig. 3.1: Usage of Cloud Computing

For example, as we increase the size of the registers used in a computer, the memory size also needs to grow and the software should be able to exploit this power effectively. Therefore, changes in hardware, networking and operating systems caused paradigms of computing to evolve reflecting the need to grow.

From one computer, we have learnt how to use multiple computers to solve large scale problems using the Internet as our communicating medium. Our applications have become more data-intensive and network-centric. All these have helped to solve larger computational problems that have become the need of the day

Web hosting is the mechanism of providing space in the World Wide Web (WWW) to host one's web resources. However, such service offerings suffered from the problem of scalability, which was mitigated by the user of virtualization. The ability to grow and shrink if required, is known as **scalability**. With the advent of computing technology, we need to have scalability that will accommodate the changes.

Scenario Prior to Cloud Computing

Prior to cloud computing, users of computing devices are supposed to invest money on computing resources such as hardware, software, networking, and storage. This investment costs a lot of money for its users as they have to buy these computing resources, keep them in their premises, and maintaining them to make them operational. And this upfront cost will become a huge expenditure to an organization that requires enormous computing and storage resources.

In traditional on-premise model, the consumer is responsible for purchasing and maintaining all of the IT infrastructure. This can be a significant upfront cost, but it can also give the consumer more control over their IT environment. There are also ongoing costs associated with staffing, hardware and software maintenance, and facilities maintenance.

In cloud computing model, the provider manages most of the IT infrastructure. This includes purchasing and maintaining hardware, software, data centre space, power, cooling, and IT staff. Cloud users typically pay a monthly fee for the resources they use.

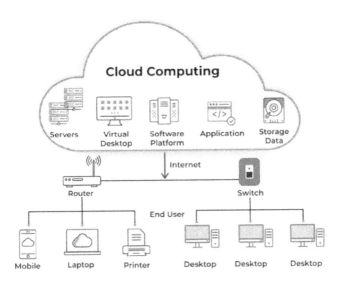

Fig. 3.2: Cloud Computing Paradigm

In cloud computing, users of computing devices such as storage and computation (CPU) can avail them from a service provider called Cloud Service Provider (CSP) as and when needed and pay only for the duration of their usage. This would cost only a reasonable investment or spending, compared to the huge investment required for buying the entire computing infrastructure.

Motivation for Cloud Computing:

The cloud represents Internet-based computing resources which are made available to the general public or an individual through some secured network connectivity. In this model of computing, an organization's core computing power resides offsite and is essentially subscribed to rather than owned. Now-a-days, cloud computing is growing in popullarity, especially among individuals, and Small and Medium Enterprises (SMEs).

Cloud computing has the power to bring the computing resources (CPU, storage etc.) to an organization or an individual without the need for capital investment, just by hiring them online from a service provider and paying only for the consumed services. Therefore, cloud computing is needed in getting the services of computing resources at the user level at an operational cost. This results in saving a lot of money by eliminating the upfront cost - cost involved in setting up and running IT resources on the premise.

In the traditional on-premise model, the consumer is responsible for purchasing and maintaining all of the IT infrastructure. This can be a significant upfront cost, but it can also give the consumer more control over their IT environment. There are also ongoing costs associated with staffing, hardware and software maintenance, and facilities maintenance.

On the other hand, in cloud computig model, the provider manages most of the IT infrastructure. This includes purchasing and maintaining hardware, software, data center space, power, cooling, and IT staff. Users typically pay a monthly fee for the resources they use.

Need for Cloud Computing:

In an organisation, cloud computing is needed in getting the services of computing resources at the user level at an operational cost. This results in saving a lot of money by eliminating the upfront cost - cost involved in setting up and running IT resources on the premise. Cloud computing encompasses the subscription based or pay-as-you-go service model for offering computing to end users or customers over the Internet and thereby extending the IT's existing capabilities.

Cloud computing makes our life easy in the field of computing by providing resources available on the computer over the Internet . As end users, we need to know how to tap into the resources available on the cloud through a system which is connected to Internet. Reliability is another major benefit of using cloud computing in our day to day lives. On the cloud, losing our data/file is much less likely. However, just like anything online, there is always a risk that someone may try to gain access to our personal data.

In the simplest terms, **cloud computing** is a kind of distributed computing in which storage and processing of data or application take place over the Internet on a remote machine instead of doing them on the local machine. The term cloud is just a metaphor for the Internet in this definition.

When we store and run a program from the local computer's hard drive, that scenario is called on premise storage and computation. That means, we have our own resources such as CPU and storage device for performing computation and storage on premise. Whereas, in cloud computing users are allowed to store and process data or programs on a computer running remotely (on the cloud) over the Internet.

Cloud Computing Paradigm

Here is a simple definition of Cloud Computing: "**Cloud Computing is a type of Computing System In which High Performance Computing resources (such as servers, application and networking) are available to its users over the Internet.**" With an online connection, cloud resources such as computing power (CPU), storage capacity (hard disk), networking features and application software such as ERP can be availed from anywhere, anytime and at any device.

According to the National Institute of Standards and Technology (NIST), **cloud computing is a model for enabling ubiquitous, convenient, on-demand network access to a shared pool of configurable computing resources (e.g networks, servers, storage, applications and services) that can be rapidly provisioned and released with minimal management effort or service provider interaction** (Mell & Grance, 2011).

At its most basic level, the Cloud provides the following basic capabilities:

- On-demand self-service
- Broad network access
- Resource pooling
- Rapid elasticity
- Measured service

Pros and Cons of using Cloud:

Cloud computing offers a number of advantages over traditional on-premise deployments. However, there are also some disadvantages to consider. The decision of whether to move to the cloud is a complex one that should be made on a case-by-case basis.

<u>**Here are the Advantages of using a Cloud Service:**</u>

Cost Savings: Cloud services are generally less expensive than on-premise deployments. This is because you don't need to purchase and maintain your own hardware and software.

Velocity/Agility: Cloud services can be provisioned much more quickly than on-premise systems. This is because the cloud provider already has the infrastructure in place.

Elasticity: Cloud services can scale up and down based on demand. This means that you only pay for the resources you use.

Security: Cloud providers generally have more resources to invest in security than most businesses. This means that your data may be more secure in the cloud than on-premise.

Here are some Disadvantages of using the Cloud:

Service Disruptions: Cloud services are reliant on the internet. If there is an internet outage, you may not be able to access your data or applications.

Privacy: Your data is stored on the cloud provider's servers. This means that you may have less control over your data than you would with an on-premise deployment.

Shift of Control: When you move to the cloud, you are giving up some control over your IT infrastructure. This means that you are relying on the cloud provider to provide a good service.

Security: Security breaches can impact multiple organizations that are using the same cloud provider.

CHAPTER FOUR

CLOUD DELIVERY & DEPLOYMENT MODELS

Infrastructure as a Service (IaaS), Platform as a Service (PaaS) and Software as a Service (SaaS) are the three major categories of services provided on the cloud for the benefit of general public.

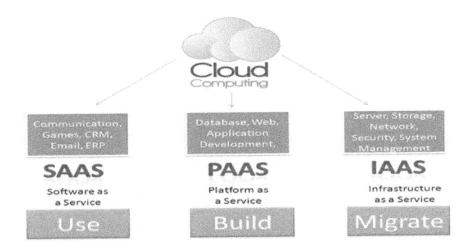

Fig. 4.1: Major Service Models of Cloud Computing

Infrastructure as a Service (IaaS):

In the Infrastructure as a Service (IaaS) delivery model, a cloud provider is providing infrastructure for consumption via the Internet. This service delivery model is delivered via Public, Private, Hybrid, and Community Cloud deployment models.

The IaaS model enables a cloud provider to provide a complete infrastructure via the Internet and enables companies to eliminate the need to maintain their own IT infrastructure such as data centers, hardware, and telecommunications links. Companies such as Netflix use public IaaS providers like Amazon Web Services (AWS).

IaaS models enable even the smallest organizations with very small IT budgets to offer a robust infrastructure for customers, which was not possible previously. IaaS enables organizations to rapidly deploy new applications/services, migrate existing services out of on-premise data centers, and introduce automation technologies to improve service delivery.

aaS enables organizations to rapidly deploy new applications/services, migrate existing services out of on-premise data centers, and introduce automation technologies to improve service delivery.

Platform as a Service (PaaS):

In a Platform as a Service (PaaS) delivery model, a cloud provider is providing a platform for customers to develop, run, and manage software applications without needing to worry about the infrastructure that normally would be required. PaaS is provided for consumption via the Internet. Although this service delivery model is most commonly delivered via a Public Cloud deployment, it could be delivered via a Private Cloud or Hybrid Cloud as well.

The PaaS model enables a cloud provider to provide a platform that can be used for rapid application development via the Internet. A company can develop and deploy an application much faster on the PaaS model, because the PaaS provider manages a significant portion of the technology stack, thus freeing the developer to focus on the application itself.

Examples of PaaS

* Heroku
* Amazon AWS

- RedHat OpenShift
- Google App Engine

Software as s Service (SaaS):

In a Software as a Service (SaaS) delivery model, a cloud provider is providing software for consumption via the Internet. Although this service delivery model is most commonly delivered via a Public Cloud deployment, it could be delivered via a Private Cloud or Hybrid Cloud as well.

	Enterprise	Small Business	Consumer
Finance	Oracle, SAP	NetSuite, Quickbooks	Mint
Sales	Salesforce, Oracle	Zoho CRM	N/A
Productivity	Microsoft Office 365, Google Docs	Microsoft Office 365, Google Docs	Microsoft Office 365, Google Docs
File Storage	Google Drive, Box	Box, Google Drive	Dropbox, iCloud, Google Drive

Fig. 4.2: Examples of SaaS Delivery of Cloud Computing

The SaaS model enables a cloud provider to provide a piece of software via the Internet, using either web browsers or native client applications, such as for mobile devices or a PC. If a client application is used, it is most likely a thin client and generally connects to a backend application programming interface (API) over HTTPS for much or all of the application functionality.

SaaS software is very common for enterprise, small business, and consumer software, and many large software companies now offer their applications under a SaaS delivery model.

Three Delivery Models of Cloud Computing

The three major deployment models of cloud computing are:

1. Public
2. Private
3. Hybrid

The Public Cloud Model:

In a public cloud deployment model, a cloud provider has services available for consumption by the general public. These services exist on infrastructure owned by the cloud provider, which may be a private entity such as a business or non-profit, or a public entity such as a government or academic institution.

Benefits

- Pay-as-you-go
- Low initial cost
- Very elastic

The cloud provider handles managing all aspects of its infrastructure, thus eliminating the need for individual companies to need to worry about any of the following infrastructure-related costs:

- Data Center Facilities
- Telecommunications lines
- Computer, storage, and networking equipment
- IT staffing such as data center technicians, network engineers, storage engineers, server engineers, systems administrators, network operations, and layers of management

Amazon Web Services (AWS) and Microsoft Azure are examples of public cloud providers for both Infrastructure as a Service (IaaS) and Platform as a Service (PaaS). Salesforce and Oracle are examples of public cloud providers for Software as a Service (SaaS) in the enterprise applications space. Dropbox, iCloud, and Google Docs are examples of public cloud providers for Software as a Service (SaaS) in the consumer and small business applications space.

he table given below outlines how a variety of businesses benefit from the availability of Public Cloud infrastructure.

Company	Profile	Public Cloud Cost	Traditional IT On-Premise Cost	Cost Savings
Company A – Tax Preparation	Peak usage: Jan-May	$28,500/year	$60,000/year	$31,500/year
Company B – Internet Retailer	Peak usage: Nov and Dec	$26,000/year	$120,000/year	$94,000/year
Company C – Video Streaming	Level usage throughout the year, but needs ability to peak traffic	$312,000/year	$480,000/year	$168,000/year
Company D – Online Summer School	Peak usage: June-Sept	$4,800/year	$12,000/year	$7,200/year

Fig. 4.3: Cost Benefit from Public Cloud Model

The Private Cloud Model:

In a private cloud deployment model, an internal department (typically called IT) has services available for consumption by other organizations within a larger organization. These services exist on infrastructure owned by the organization, which may be a private entity such as a business or non-profit, or a public entity such as a government or academic institution.

Benefits

- Complete control over implementation and management
- Completely customizable
- Security

The department running the private cloud handles managing all aspects of its infrastructure, thus eliminating the need for individual organizations to need to worry about any of the following infrastructure-related costs:

- Data Center Facilities
- Telecommunications lines
- Computer, storage, and networking equipment
- IT staffing such as data center technicians, network engineers, storage engineers, server engineers, systems administrators, network operations, and layers of management

The table given below outlines how a variety of organizations benefit from the availability of Private Cloud infrastructure.

Organization	Profile	Private Cloud Cost	Traditional IT On-Premise Cost	Cost Savings
Tax Department	Peak usage: Jan-May	$28,500/year	$60,000/year	$31,500/year
Payroll	Peak usage: 1st and 15th of each month	$12,000/year	$120,000/year	$108,000/year
Sales and Marketing	Level usage throughout the year, but needs ability to peak traffic	$12,000/year	$120,000/year	$108,000/year
Human Resources	Peak usage: During annual reviews in December	$4,800/year	$24,000/year	$19,200/year

Fig. 4.4: Cost Benefits from Private Cloud Model

OpenStack and Apache CloudStack are examples of open-source private cloud solutions, whereas vCloud and Microsoft Private Cloud are examples of commercial private cloud solutions for Infrastructure as a Service (IaaS).

The Hybrid Cloud Model:

In a hybrid cloud deployment model, an organization uses both public and private cloud solutions and implements management frameworks to enable workload interoperability.

Benefits

- Elasticity to meet peak workloads

- Internal IT staff can manage both environments at different levels to meet business needs
- Workloads can be moved to the appropriate cloud platform based on the organization's criteria
- Low risk without sacrificing agility

Hybrid Cloud Case Study

A Big Company Corporation (ABC Corp.) is a global organization with a large in-house IT infrastructure. The company decides to shift all infrastructures to the cloud to reduce costs and complexity as well as reduce the need for IT staff in each department, but worries about placing sensitive systems in the public cloud. Jane, the CIO, has proposed using a hybrid cloud deployment model, with most baseline workloads running in a private cloud, but with the ability for certain peak workloads to automatically scale-out to the public cloud. This approach will enable the organization to reduce overall IT costs and complexity, while still meeting business requirements.

Services Offered by Amazon

Amazon Web Services (AWS) offers a broad set of cloud-based products and services to its users. Some of the key services provided by AWS include:

Compute Services: This category includes services like Amazon Elastic Compute Cloud (EC2) for scalable virtual servers, AWS Lambda for serverless computing, and Amazon Elastic Container Service (ECS) for container management.

Storage Services: AWS provides various storage options such as Amazon Simple Storage Service (S3) for object storage, Amazon Elastic Block Store (EBS) for block storage, and Amazon Glacier for long-term data archiving.

Database Services: Users can leverage services like Amazon Relational Database Service (RDS) for managed relational databases, Amazon DynamoDB for NoSQL databases, and Amazon Redshift for data warehousing.

Analytics Services: AWS offers services like Amazon Athena for interactive query analysis, Amazon EMR for big data processing, and Amazon Kinesis for real-time data streaming.

Networking Services: Users can utilize services such as Amazon Virtual Private Cloud (VPC) for isolated cloud resources, Amazon Route 53 for domain name system (DNS) management, and AWS Direct Connect for dedicated network connections.

Developer Tools: AWS provides tools like AWS CodeCommit for source control, AWS CodeBuild for continuous integration, and AWS CodeDeploy for automated application deployment.

Management Tools: Users can benefit from services like AWS CloudFormation for infrastructure as code, AWS CloudWatch for monitoring and logging, and AWS Systems Manager for managing resources at scale.

Security Services: AWS offers services such as AWS Identity and Access Management (IAM) for access control, AWS Key Management Service (KMS) for encryption key management, and Amazon GuardDuty for threat detection.

Internet of Things (IoT): AWS provides IoT services like AWS IoT Core for device connectivity, AWS IoT Greengrass for local computing, and AWS IoT Device Management for managing IoT devices.

Enterprise Applications: Users can access services like Amazon WorkSpaces for virtual desktops, Amazon WorkDocs for secure document storage, and Amazon Chime for online meetings.

These are just a few examples of the extensive range of services offered by AWS to help users build, deploy, and manage applications in the cloud.

CHAPTER FIVE

DATA CENTER AND VIRTUALIZATION

Shifting an organization's IT needs from a traditional on-premise model to a cloud model requires an analysis of the potential economic implications.

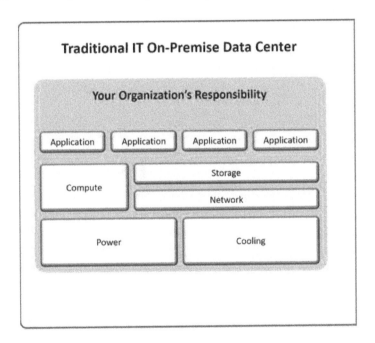

Figure 5.1: Traditional On-Premise IT Infrasture

All organizations, whether they are for profit, nonprofit, or government, have finite budgets. Management must allocate these finite financial assets appropriately so that the leaders can make sound business decisions and meet the objectives of the organization.

Information Technology (IT) is a key strategic function to help support the objectives of an organization. Businesses first used information systems to replace paper-based methods of helping management perform these functions, and that use continues today. Managers must be able to understand different IT models to make the best financial investment decisions for the organization.

Cloud platforms utilize virtualization technologies to carve up large pools of hardware resources into smaller chunks, which can be utilized and allocated to a consumer.Virtualization is a technique allowing computers to effectively emulate other computers as well as various hardware devices.

Virtualization was developed in the 1960s to provide compatibility between computer mainframes and it has evolved into today's modern version where a standard server machine (host) can emulate multiple machines of various types and sizes.

Data Centers in Cloud Computing

In a Cloud environment, the data center infrastructure is abstracted from the consumer's view. Systems such as power, cooling, computer hardware, storage hardware, and network hardware are invisible to the consumer. These cloud data centers are large buildings, located with access to multiple power supplies, and located in areas with significant networking capacity. The infrastructure of these facilities employs standardized layouts for equipment racks, networking equipment, power supplies, and cooling.

Cloud Compute:

Cloud compute refers to a variety of server resources where an application workload may run, such as: virtualized, containers, or bare-metal. In a cloud model, these compute resources may span many physical devices and locations. In addition, these compute resources are provisioned programmatically.

Cloud Storage:

Cloud storage refers to a model where data is stored in logical storage pools, spanning many physical devices and locations. A consumer of a cloud storage service does not have any visibility or control over where their data is stored.

Software Defined Network:

Software Defined Networking (SDN) is a set of techniques to create abstract interfaces to networking protocols and hardware devices, and implement them in software so that networks for virtual resources in the cloud can be programmatically created, configured, maintained, and controlled.

In Software Defined Networking, the network infrastructure control function is separated from the low-level implementation using dynamic, cost-effective, and programmatically manageable methods.

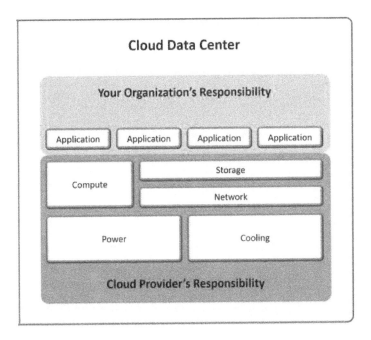

Fig. 5.2: Cloud Computing Infrasture

The diagrams shown in Fig. 5.2 shows a cloud data center (assuming an IaaS service delivery model), and the responsibility of both the Cloud Provider and Cloud User in managing the resources available in it.

Software Defined Data Center:

Software Defined Data Center (SDDC) is in its simplest form a pool of resources (i.e. storage, network, compute, etc.) that can be provisioned, configured, and discovered dynamically based on workload requirements.

In a Software Defined Data Center, the concepts of virtualization, automated provisioning, control, and management are extended to all aspects of data center infrastructure, making it completely available as a service.

Virtualization in Cloud Computing

Virtualization allows for software emulation of all kinds of hardware devices. It enables creation of software defined environments in which various components of computer systems can be virtualized. It is one of the main enabling technologies of cloud computing.

An important fact about virtualization is that virtual components, defined and run by the software, can be programmatically provisioned and controlled, allowing for high level of automation of the cloud.

Open Source	Commercial
Linux KVM	VMWare
Xen	Microsoft HyperV
VirtualBox	Oracle Solaris Containers

Fig. 5.3: Open Source and Commercial Virtualization Software

The software which allows virtualization is called hypervisor. The emulated machines are called virtual machines or virtual servers. Hypervisor can run directly on the server's hardware substituting for the host's operating system, and each virtual server running its own operating system and applications (type 1 hypervisor or sometimes called bare-metal hypervisor).

Alternatively, it can run on top of the host's native operating system (type 2 hypervisor or sometimes called hosted hypervisor) taking advantage of its features but inserting an extra layer in the software stack.

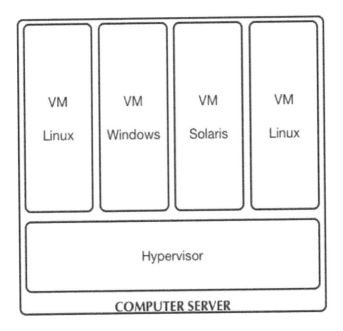

Fig. 5.4: The Role of Hypervisor in Virtualization

Steps involved in Setting up a Virtual Machine (VM):

This optional and ungraded lab walks you through setting up VirtualBox on your computer, so that you can run virtualized environments. Please confirm that your computer has sufficient resources such as memory (RAM), CPU, and disk space before attempting this lab.

1. Download the appropriate version of VirtualBox for your computer and follow the instructions provided with the installer to install onto your computer.

2. After installation, you can start VirtualBox as follows:

- On Windows, go to "Programs" and then click on "VirtualBox".
- On macOS, go to "Applications" and double-click on "VirtualBox".
- On Linux or Solaris, you can type VirtualBox into a terminal window.

3. Decide whether you wish to install a pre-built developer VM, or create a new VM from scratch using an operating system that you may have such as Windows, or an operating system that you can download from the Internet such as Linux.

4. If you wish to create a new VM from scratch, please skip to **Step 6**.

5. There are a variety of different VM's, but you may wish to consider the OpenStack for Linux if you would like to explore building out your own Private Cloud lab. Each VM contains instructions for installing the VM in VirtualBox.

6. If you choose to create a new VM from scratch, please click **New** at the top of the VirtualBox Manager window. A wizard will guide you through the setup of your first virtual machine (VM)

7. After you have created your VM, you may start it by double-clicking in the **VirtualBox Manager** window, or selecting it in the **Manager** window and pressing **Start**.

8. If you chose to create a new VM, then you will need to use the **First Start Wizard** to install your operating system.

9. After your VM's operating system is installed, then you will be able to access that VM in a window on your computer.

CHAPTER SIX

Cloud Economics

The financial requirements for the cloud computing model are vastly different than the financial requirements for an on-premise model.

Type	Cloud Model	Traditional IT On-Premise Model
Data center real estate	No	Yes
Data center power and cooling	No	Yes
Data center management	No	Yes
Vendor/Contract management	Yes	Yes
IT Staffing - Datacenter support	No	Yes
IT Staffing - Network/Storage/Servers Support	No	Yes
IT Staffing - Application Engineers	Maybe	Yes
IT Staffing - Cloud Engineers (multi-purpose roles)	Yes	No
IT Staffing - Database Engineers	Maybe	Yes
IT Staffing - NOC	No	Yes
IT Staffing - Security Engineers	Maybe	Yes
Software	Maybe	Yes
Telecommunications	Maybe	Yes
Hardware	No	Yes
Cloud Hosting Subscriptions	Yes	No
Professional Services	Maybe	Maybe

Figure 6.1: Cloud Vs On-Premise Model Cost Comparison

In a traditional IT on-premise model, your organization would be responsible for either operating your own data center, or procuring services from a colocation provider. This would require that you either operate an entire data center facility yourself, or rent physical space in an existing colocation facility. Either way, you will incur costs (such as: power, cooling, real estate, equipment, staffing, and telecommunications) that are entirely borne by you either directly for a data center facility, or indirectly for a colocation facility.

The staffing and other costs associated with maintaining and operating a data center facility with high availability are very large, and as a result colocation facilities are an alternative that may be considered. These colocation facilities provide rental of space, power, cooling, and telecommunications from a company operating an existing data center facility. With colocation, you are still responsible for installing, maintaining, and operating all hardware and software, which means that you will still have significant IT staffing costs. Either way, in an on-premise model you are responsible for every component in the technology stack.

Economies of Scale:

One of the benefits of cloud computing is the ability to take advantage of economies of scale. Cloud service providers provide a large-scale platform to a number of different clients, which reduces the unit cost that each client pays.

In a traditional on-premise IT model, each organization has to invest in data center facilities, telecommunications links, network infrastructure, servers, storage, staffing, applications, and databases. Under a cloud computing model, an organization can simply rent these items from an organization that invests in these items on a much larger scale.

The costs associated with operating in a cloud model can be vastly different than those associated with operating in a traditional IT on-premises model. Cloud computing shifts IT budgets to a pure operating expense model, whereas the traditional on-premise computing model requires both capital and operating expense allocations.

In a cloud model, your organization is generally only responsible for the following for each cloud service delivery model consumed:
IaaS

- Applications
- Databases
- Frameworks / Application Servers

PaaS

- Applications

SaaS

- Nothing (your organization is just a consumer of someone else's application)

In other words, if you consume a SaaS service, then you generally have no responsibility for any portion of the technology stack. You are simply a user of the service, and your organization can expect the cloud provider to own the entire technology stack. There may be some complex situations, particularly in the enterprise SaaS space, where you are provided a stock application instance, and then have to customize the application for your unique business needs.

Overview of IT Budgeting

The IT budgeting process varies from organization to organization, but most organizations allocate their budget into two areas: Capital Expenses, and Operating Expenses.

Capital Expenses (CapEx):

A capital expense, often abbreviated as CAPEX, is an economic cost related to acquiring or upgrading tangible or intangible capital assets.
Examples of capital assets include:

- Tangible assets such as real estate, manufacturing equipment, computers, and office furniture
- Intangible assets such as copyrights, intellectual property, and product patents

In terms of cloud computing, CAPEX usually refers to the cost of acquiring and/or upgrading a private data center hosting the organization's technology equipment such as servers, storage, and network equipment, as well as the actual acquisition of that equipment.

In a traditional IT environment, an organization will have capital expenses for the following:

Data center facilities and onsite server rooms includes: Air conditioning systems, power generators, uninterruptable power supplies (batteries), cabling, power distribution units, HVAC ductwork, racks, and specialized fire suppression systems.

Server, storage, and network hardware includes: routers, switches, firewalls, intrusion detection and protection systems, load balancers, rackmount servers, blade servers, specialized computing appliances, storage area network (SAN), network attached storage (NAS), direct attached storage (DAS), storage networking equipment, tape libraries and drives, disk-based backup systems, etc.

Software includes: database software, application software, operating systems software, and utility software.

Operating Expenditure (OpEx):

An operating expense, often abbreviated OPEX, is an economic cost incurred by a business through normal business operations.

Examples of operating expenses include:

- Cloud hosting
- Mortgage and rent
- Inventory costs
- Office equipment and manufacturing machinery (such as maintenance, support, etc.)
- Payroll costs
- Marketing costs
- Money used for research and development (R&D)

Note: sometimes R&D costs are treated as CAPEX by an organization. For the purposes of this course, we treat R&D as an operating expense.

IT Budgeting Process:

Most organizations adopt a top-down budgeting approach, which means that the corporate executives set high-level enterprise budgets and pass those down to the department heads. The IT department head then takes the high-level budget number for IT, and works with IT management to determine how the organization's IT budget will be allocated. Typically, this IT budget will be divided into capital and operating expense budgets.

Example:

- Your CEO provides your CIO with a $10 million operating expense budget, and a $4 million capital expense budget.
- Your CIO has to carve up that $10 million in operating expenses, to cover expenses such as: IT staffing, leasing employee workstations, and external hosting costs. Your CIO also has to carve up that $4 million in capital expenses, to cover items such as: data center investments, storage, servers, and networking equipment.

Using AWS Cloud Calculator

The Amazon Web Services Simple Monthly Calculator provides a relatively simple method for obtaining a cost estimate for Amazon services, and enables you to generate an estimate of your monthly bill by playing with different parameters. This is a good tool for understanding your potential direct cloud subscription costs on Amazon, but will not provide you with your total cost of ownership (TCO) for moving to the cloud.

The Amazon Web Services TCO Calculator provides a relatively simple method for obtaining a cost estimate for Amazon services, and enables you to compare against either an on-premises (where you completely run your own data center facility), and colocation (where you install your own hardware in a facility owned by someone else). This is a good tool for comparing the traditional IT economics model against the cloud economics model.

The calculators provide an easy-to-use interface for entering data for your scenario and creating a cost estimate for you. The interface is as simple as clicking to select values in fields, and entering additional data using your keyboard.

These calculators provide a much more accurate picture of actual costs than you would find on your own, because the vendors constantly update the pricing models based on their own pricing and competitor trends. Try to learn how to use the Amazon Web Services calculator to compare cloud and on-premise hosting costs.

Consider the Scenario:

Your management has come to you in a panic, because your IT budget is out of control. The company is growing revenue at a rapid pace, but the cost of your IT infrastructure is outpacing that growth and profit margins are at risk. You have been asked to calculate what it would cost to move your existing IT infrastructure to the cloud, and compare with your existing on-premise costs. For the ease of computations, you will assume that Amazon's costs for an equivalent on-premise environment are accurate.

You currently have the following systems:

- 10 DB Virtual Machines with 16 cores each, 64gb RAM each, running on VMware hypervisors, and running Oracle SE1 (LI)
- 100 Non-DB Virtual Machines with 4 cores each, 16gb RAM each, running on VMware hypervisors, and running Linux
- 100 TB of SAN storage
- 100 TB of NAS storage
- 1000 TB of Object storage, with 80% access infrequently

Instructions to Use the Calculator:

1. Open your web browser, and go to: https://calculator.aws/
2. For currency, select "United States Dollar"
3. For environment, select "On-Premises"
4. For AWS region, select "US East"
5. For workload type, select "General"
6. For physical or virtual, select "Virtual Machines"

7. In the "Servers" section, enter the parameters for non-DB virtual machines from the above scenario into the appropriate fields
8. Click on "Add Row"
9. Repeat for the DB Virtual machines
10. In the "Storage" section, enter the parameters for SAN storage from the above scenario into the appropriate fields
11. Click on "Add Row"
12. Repeat for the NAS storage
13. Click on "Add Row"
14. Repeat for the Object storage
15. Click on "Calculate TCO"

Cloud Total Cost of Ownership:

The Total cost of ownership (TCO) in the context of IT is a financial measure used to understand all costs (direct and indirect) for providing IT services. As you consider shifting to the cloud you will want to understand all costs associated with such a shift, as opposed to just the easily visible costs, such as the monthly cloud subscription fees.

In addition, TCO will vary from organization to organization, based on the specifics of your type of organization. In this unit, you will look at some costs that make up the total cost of ownership for the cloud model. We will also explore how the type of organization can affect TCO and we will wrap up by providing the resources needed for you to develop a TCO model for your organization.

The following costs may need to be considered for your cloud total cost of ownership analysis:

- Cloud hosting subscription fees
- Application software licenses
- Migration expenses
- Cloud domain-specific staffing expenses
- Development expenses
- Payments to customers for outages
- Existing investments in on-premise infrastructure
- Existing staffing expenses, including severance payments
- Professional service expenses

- Risks such as:

  - Exposure to security vulnerabilities
  - Availability of upgrades and patches
  - Future third-party licensing costs
  - Cloud provider insolvency
  - Natural disasters
  - System downtime
  - Performance
  - Backup and recovery
  - Training
  - Cloud provider price shifts
  - Testing

www.ingramcontent.com/pod-product-compliance
Lightning Source LLC
Chambersburg PA
CBHW041638050326
40690CB00026B/5266